ARCHING INTO THE AFTERLIFE

Bilingual Press/Editorial Bilingüe

General Editor
    Gary D. Keller

Managing Editor
    Karen S. Van Hooft

Senior Editor
    Mary M. Keller

Associate Editor
    Ann M. Waggoner

Assistant Editor
    Julia C. Angelica

Editorial Board
    Juan Goytisolo
    Francisco Jiménez
    Eduardo Rivera
    Severo Sarduy
    Mario Vargas Llosa

Address:
Bilingual Review/Press
Hispanic Research Center
Arizona State University
Tempe, Arizona 85287
(602) 965-3867

ARCHING INTO THE AFTERLIFE

Pablo Medina

Bilingual Press/Editorial Bilingüe
TEMPE, ARIZONA

ISBN 0-927534-12-6

Library of Congress Cataloging-in-Publication Data

Medina, Pablo, 1948-
    Arching into the afterlife / by Pablo Medina.
        p.   cm.
    Includes bibliographical references.
    ISBN 0-927534-12-6 (pbk.)
    I. Title.
  PS3563.E24A89   1991
  811'.54—dc20   90-24943
                                                   CIP

PRINTED IN THE UNITED STATES OF AMERICA

Front cover photograph of Joseph Stella's *The Voice of the City of New York Interpreted: The Bridge* 1920-22, Collection of the Newark Museum, Purchase 1937, Felix Fuld Bequest Fund. Armen Photographers.

Cover design by Kerry Curtis

Back cover photo by Lou Draper

Acknowledgments

Grateful acknowledgment is given to the following periodicals in which some of these poems have appeared:

The Americas Review (17.2, 1989), *Arab Perspectives* (1.6, 1980), *Black Swan Review* (2, 1989), *Contact II* (6.34/35, 1984/1985), *Hubbub* (4.2, 1986), *Kansas Quarterly* (19.3, 1987), *Linden Lane Magazine* (1.4, 1982), *Miami Monthly* (9.9, 9.12, 1989), *Milkweed Chronicle* (1.3, 1980), *The Palmetto Review* (4, 1986), *Passaic Review* (7/8, 1985), *Paterson Literary Review* (1989), *Poet Lore* (79.1, 1984), *The Spirit That Moves Us* (4.1, 1978/79), *Stone Country* (10.3/4, 1983), *Tar River Poetry* (25.1, 1985), *Terra Poetica* (2.1/2, 1983), *US 1 Worksheets* (6/7, 1978; 16/17, 1983/84; 18/19, 1985; 22/23, 1989).

(Acknowledgments continue on page 84.)

I gratefully acknowledge the Oscar B. Cintas Foundation, the New Jersey State Council on the Arts and the Pennsylvania Council on the Arts for their financial assistance.

I also wish to thank the following persons who kept me on the path: Dan Aubrey, James Haba, Carolina Hospital, Belkis Cuza Malè, Heberto Padilla, Gregory Orfalea, my parents, and especially my son, Pablo A. Medina, wise beyond his years.

Also by Pablo Medina

Pork Rind and Cuban Songs

Exiled Memories: A Cuban Childhood

*Everyone Will Have to Listen/Todos me van
a tener que oír: The Poetry of Tania Díaz Castro*
(edited and translated with Carolina Hospital)

CONTENTS

*for María Cecilia Gray,
Karen Gordon, and Ellen Jacko*

*What punishment is this
that glitters so?*

—Dante, *The Inferno*

The Courage of the Poet

Gregory Orfalea

It is fitting that Pablo Medina's work is beginning to reach a wider audience, though it has been well received in New Jersey where he has taught for sixteen years, and in the Cuban exile communities of Miami and the eastern seaboard. Along with the publication of his memoirs, *Exiled Memories: A Cuban Childhood*, and his first novel, *The Marks of Birth*, a second collection of poems has been fifteen years in the making. Reader, you must gather your forces. Though it is a book of uncommon beauty, *Arching into the Afterlife* is nothing short of a descent into hell.

Pablo Medina was born in Havana, Cuba, in 1948, to a family of merchants and intellectuals. His childhood was filled with the simple pleasures and mysteries of the tropics—glistening waters, fecund swamps, cane fields redolent of sugar and human sweat. His grandfather, Pablo Medina I, was an eclectic genius, a commentator on Cuban radio and early television. Cherished musicologist as well as regular participant in the popular Cuban version of the "$64,000 Question," "La Bolsa del Saber," Grandfather Pablo's erudition had a big impact on the grandson: "His opinions would be punctuated with quotes from and allusions to Shakespeare, Cervantes, Aristotle, the Koran, and any other source that might pop into his head." His commentaries were published in a book, *Medinadas.* But the man with the huge portrait of Beethoven in his living room whose "stormy gaze fell on every corner" was something of a profligate. When he fled his marriage and died away from the family, the grandson "went to the grove by the chicken coop. . . . There, away from everyone, I cried for him whom I had known so little, and I cried for myself, feeling for the first time the gray milk of mortality spreading over everything until there was nothing but solitude and a dark, moonless night" (*Exiled Memories: A Cuban Childhood*, 1990, pp. 67, 76). And thus the theme of joy killed by separation appeared in the grandson's own work.

In 1960, the Medina family left Cuba, ushering both the young son and his sister into the startling snow world of New York City. Snow would become a Medina obsession: "cold and brillant as the hand of God." The father worked as an importer of Spanish perfumes, the bottled essence of flower. It was as if the Medina family could not let go of the odor of the island. The son came of age in the Bronx and the subways trying to square snow with perfume: a poet's calling.

After attending Fordham Prep and Georgetown University, where he received degrees in English and Spanish, Medina took jobs as various as courier for a passport agency and counter of rush-hour cars for the Highway Department. (No doubt his hatred of bureaucracies stems partly from that experience.) With the publication of *Pork Rind and Cuban Songs* (1975)—the first book of poems written in English by a Cuban exile—Medina came to the attention of Chilean poet Nicanor Parra, who singled his work out for praise at a symposium of Spanish-American writers at Columbia University.

Filled with poems of memory, family, and Cuban and Spanish heritage, *Pork Rind* refrained from either romanticizing the revolution or those who lost much in fleeing. Bewilderment at violent social cataclysms is the chief feeling. In his classic parable, "The Taino Male's Elegy to Himself," in which the passive Taino Indian awaits his own engorgement by the cannibal Caribes, Medina offered a subtle rebuke to those who stayed for the regimentation of Castro, who "taught me / peace at the expense of my own / freedom." At the same time, Medina rubbed salt in the wounds of exiles who embraced middle-class amenities in a place where "the weeding of cuticles (is) / far more technically advanced." He saw too many exiles "drowning in the soap of memory."

Because *Pork Rind*'s publisher was short-lived, *Arching into the Afterlife* will introduce Medina's poetry to many. It is a very different and more difficult book. Not just the product of a long, gestating, and unusual critique of the nature of freedom, and of America itself, it is also a spiritual journey, one as I have mentioned, through madness and hell. A Cuban element is almost nonexistent, with the exception of the last section with its sad longing, "The girl with the wide hips wades into the sea / coconut milk in her groin, lilac / lips as close to truth as ever were." But Medina is after bigger game than ethnicity. The very title itself evokes a wrenching leap at transcendence. He is stalking the Creator who all too often answers with "the dark deafening slap of silence."

The book opens with a foreboding meditation on Rodin's "The Gates of Hell," where "No one knows what is beyond them / or when they will open / or if he's already in." The journey through four carefully constructed sections spirals ever downward through what appear to be four stages of despair. The first section explores the Hell of the Mind, the second a Hell of Society (what Carthage was to Augustine, Trenton, New Jersey, is to Medina), the third a Hell of Love (hell because of spent promise and drowned will—the beloved is "lost beyond the river / where trucks devour children"). The fourth section is a coda of sorts containing elegies to dead Cubans, yet a "thrust of hope."

Consciousness, Medina tells us at the beginning, is a "bite." It is almost as if life itself were a feverish attempt to develop an antitoxin to the excesses of the plundering ego:

> Learn to recognize the pride
> we bring to peristyles
> and colonnades. It crumbles.
> Learn the pieces falling.
> Make room in the heart:
> the moon dye spills.

In Medina we find a constant tension between despair and hope, between the insensate and the blessing of empathy.

The poet's role is marked at the start with "God's face receding," from a land "full of innocence / and comfortable slumber." He is, in a word, an apostate: "To breathe fire / in this land is a conspiracy / of wrong." But fire the poet must breathe to awaken the world (and himself) from deadly indifference and helplessness.

A landscape littered with "three thousand cars abandoned on the roads," where "oil slicks the back of morning" is the bleak world Medina must traverse. But he is determined to go down "in the darkness" and across the threatening snow, as in "Crossing," a poem reminiscent of the hallucinatory winter trek of Yuri in *Dr. Zhivago* during the Russian Revolution. Pascal's *Deus Absconditus* who becomes an executive indifferent to the pervasive hell is directly addressed in "For the End of Winter," one of the most powerful poems in the book. Winter for Medina is the enemy—it is a symbol of cleanliness and removal and death. But winter is also the fire which burnishes his soul. He is, afterall, in *El Norte*.

Spring, when the "cobwebs sparkle," brings a warm wind the poet wants to believe, but it becomes the most cruel time of the year because of "separation." In Medina, cleavages are wide; his fascination with bridges—that they even "arch" to get where they must—is not accidental.

This book is an assault on the dehumanized. In "State Complex," we find that "The Temples resemble offices, the offices / resemble prisons, the prisons resemble factories." Through this scene God "slinks" like a "huge cat," as did the yellow fog in Eliot's *Prufrock*. It appears at times as if America's edifices are more alive than living organisms themselves. It is the Brooklyn Bridge which "arches into the afterlife" as fish lie dead in their boxes in front of it. I have thought at times that Medina's landscapes are an odd combination of Chagall and Edward Hopper, a kind of dreaming loneliness. In an apochryphal lyric, "Dawn over Washington," we find "Everywhere institutions. / In glass bodices, in marble corsets." When the poet hears the fountains in this deadened scene, he cries out "Freedom / more alive than you." Maybe not Chagall and Hopper—maybe Edvard Munch.

It is Medina's arresting and heretical notion that freedom has reduced, rather than enhanced, individualism. The poet is "bound to freedom," almost as if enslaved. At a time when the Soviet Union is undergoing upheavals resulting from its experimentation with democracy, it may do us well to question, as Medina does, the costs of excessive freedom. A citizenry, such as that of the United States, armed with 60 million handguns which kill 23,000 people a year is hardly at peace with itself. With his journey through the urban inferno, Medina's is a relentless inquiry into the byproducts of fear. Freedom, he seems to say, has deteriorated to "escape."

"Palm Sunday" here is not Stevens' "Sunday Morning." It is a horrifying vision. That omnivorous "You" (God or God-like authority) has "stropped the river / till it shines and tied our dreams to this dead earth / where the huge bird Freedom spreads its wings!" Liberty has clearly turned libertine. The fire of independence has become a spectral figure, and those wings feel nuclear.

"Coming to terms with emptiness / making it sweet as it trickles / down the throat"—this is Medina's fate. But his is a responsible search. For one thing, he seeks a way to preserve children, that is, the future: "The problem is that some of the children / will not dance." In viewing the ruins of a bomb, he laments that "we've left the children out again," or left them "to roam with nothing to do."

Medina's poems suggest the sense of history and crumbling civilizations one finds in C. P. Cavafy and John Haines. To Medina, little progress has been made by Progress. Viewing Jersey factories belching smoke, he imagines a "peasant with a clubfoot walking home." However fascinated with the medieval and ruins, Medina does not romanticize "the old times"; they contain their "Salomes / grunting for the pleasure of a bleeding head." But the lunge for the immediacy of earlier days rings partly ironic, "In the old times we feared ourselves." True; now, it seems, we fear something Nameless.

It should be obvious by now that Medina is an angry poet in the way of Allen Ginsberg. But if he were just angry, *Arching into the Afterlife* would toll with the leaden music of a jeremiad. It does not. As with Kierkegaard, despair is the fever from which he must "break" to garner life and hope. If Medina's themes are Eliotian, his language is dipped in the lushness of Latin America—the beauty which draws him blooms with stunning imagery. In "To the Muse" he admits, "Here on your nape is the thinnest vein / where meaning gathers." Though the sensual can be a trap (as in "The Lathe of Navels"), beauty rescues Medina at crucial moments. He gives himself over to reverie in "Cosmology For the Beloved's Leg," and declares of the foot's arch, "Whoever kisses here / will taste the rainbow / a river of veins, / dogs howling at midnight."

The inferno descends to its depths in the third section, where the poet's yearning and anger reach near orgasmic peak. It is a haunting sequence of love poems that culminates in the strange, transcendent affirmation of "Lilacs in Bloom."

Poe would have understood the anguish, though Medina's sensual imagery and music suggest Pablo Neruda's own esteemed love sequence. Medina's women take many forms. There is she whose body "was a lake flickering / with membranes and moss." One, like the Deity, is always leaving: "by goes your body arching / like twilight at dusk." In cold weather he struggles to that familiar bridge to meet her in "Landscape with a Red Bridge." There is the woman on a plane to whom he whispers, "Oh lovely professional lady / melt on my hand." Another poem hints of Eliot's "Game of Chess" section of *The Waste Land*—a courtesan "on a crimson recliner / languorous" suggests a game of poker. But it is in

"Lilacs in Bloom" that Medina pulls out all the stops, addressing both his social and amatory demons, "Baby land / who told you to grow fangs?" The poem builds into a delirium of cacophonous voices—mocking, prostrate, agonized. It is an exhausting ordeal, as trying and daring as "Howl." The ending contains a gaping caesura—several empty lines actually—and a period bizarrely placed at the beginning of a sentence toward the end of the poem. For Medina, love is indeed "the nest / under rushes by the ice-jammed river." Ecstatic as it is tragic, the lilacs he finds in "an ocean of gall" reveal that love matters—it "makes sense because it doesn't." Somehow love continues life.

Carolina Hospital, in her interesting anthology *Cuban American Writers: Los Atrevidos*, finds a commonality in them: "a willingness to go out on a limb and take risks linguistically and structurally." Add thematically for Medina. Hospital finds that Medina, in particular, reflects their "humorous and sometimes fantastical, hallucinatory world." I have not dwelt here on Medina's humor, though it is there. Nor have I explored the intricacies of his imagery, language, and fine ear. But as for Medina "not resisting," as Hospital asserts of Cuban American writers, I think he resists much—entropy, meaninglessness, the inhuman. He certainly resists exploring solely as a Cuban the land in which he came to manhood. Medina's is an odyssey of a soul exposed; there is no cloak save courage.

Arching into the Afterlife brings back brimstone from hell, but also, trembling, lilacs in bloom. In the meanest of circumstances—and perhaps an exile is better stationed to face them unflinchingly than a native son of these spoiled shores—his message resounds: *Make room in the heart.* The book evidences a courage rare in American poetry—so dominated since William Carlos Williams by narrow striptease confessionalism and bland academic notches for tenure—and a spiritual rigor evident in only a very few poets since Eliot himself. Medina is not "confessing," as lesser poets do with their agony. Far from Third World ambulance chasing, his politics are bred in the bones, tested through long experience. He hunts with pinpoint attention to immediate circumstances the root of evil and the seat of God. I have not referred to Eliot blithely. At the end of history's most murderous century, *Arching into the Afterlife* recalls *The Waste Land.* It is that original, that serious.

One

The Gates of Hell

1.

No one knows what is beyond them
or when they will open
or if he's already in.

A father gnaws at his sons,
lovers lunge outward
to escape and all the rest
boil in the knowledge of their damning.

2.

The damned give shadows so smooth,
so rounded, he who shaped them
must have known sinew,
curve and plane as he knew sin.

Every form is light
dulled into despair.
Love or its disguise leads here:
failed grasping.

Here we recognize
the moment darkness made us
bend and touch our heels,
know loss, our father's breath,
the bite of consciousness.

3.

A man ponders over us,
central, hunched,
not at peace with thought
but not in agony.

His shoulders hold a concentration,
a leveling, balance without delight,

almost a hope
that somewhere night is ebbing.

The Apostate

To breathe fire
in this land is a conspiracy
of wrong.

The moon outside
wanes over yellowing fields.

In this land
only the teeth of barking dogs
give light.

There is coffee
and phones ringing
and funereal smoke.

Na na, na na sings a girl
on the road into autumn.
She stops, she turns, she goes.

Far away behind the hills—
birth, red earth.

Behind that
God's face receding.

The land is full of innocence
and comfortable slumber.
Na na, na na.
Few birds remain. The grass
is dying. The earth turns hard.

For the End of Winter

1.

Of this I am sure:
that the boy found frozen in a mound of snow
after two weeks thought it was soft
and warm like a breast and died believing so.

That every year is a bull led to slaughter,
the same bull black and dreary in December,
white in January.

I can hear the wind whipping round
the three thousand cars abandoned on the roads.

That the crow shivers in its flight, its tears
staining the impeccable fields,
vile its enemy the white, its caw the call to shadows,
hope that from its feathers comes the antidote
against the claims of time.

Of this I am sure.

2.

Where am I?
in the darkness.

Where my past?
In the darkness.

Where my dreams of Light Everlasting
and warm gloves?
In the darkness.

Where my love, dulce et tremolo?
In the darkness.

And the door to Paradise and Peace?
In the darkness.

And the Voice of Voices?
In the darkness:

Pitch
Crowspit
Bullsnout
Mystery of closet afternoons
in the darkness:
                    covered by snow.

3.

Blind longing like a hurricane in the groin
tried to sift nature and put rings on the nostrils of the age;

blind led to a thousand evenings of Arctic bellies
drinking the night in like cold coffee,
while lone fishermen sang sad interminable
ballads in their dinghies buffeted by storms,

while You sat comfortable in Your divine seat
and wished not to be disturbed,

while You slept, while You ate, while You conducted
Your affairs in Your plush office, the leather couch
groaning with a numberless host of business associates;

blind with family and responsibilities and stock
in Your company, wanting to do anything You commanded,
oh for a glance or a smile or the thunder of Your voice,
and nothing came but the dark deafening slap of silence.

4.

Let slow bone powder cover my eyelids
and the fires of the Bronx singe my temples
and fat worms stifle my ears.

Let me call my lawyer and my psychiatrist
when they are never home. Let me cower in my bedroom
afraid of black hoodlums or a snowstorm that won't let

me go to work or cause my lawn to die or cause me
to die of a heart attack when I shovel the driveway.

Let the snows melt and the waters rise,
the waters rise, so that I run desperate and wild-eyed
to the next Bible meeting
but the meeting is cancelled due to bad weather

and I find myself in a dinghy rocked
by terrible waves, and I curse you and deny you
and throw all my provisions in your face

until the storm abates, the water so clear I see
no image of myself but the dolphin need
to be a wave, a vast green depth,

the flayed trees waiting for the mockingbird
to melt the tomb's shadow,
to sing holes in the sky!

Discourse on Method

The philosopher thinks
of the history of Europe,
all those centuries
like the loose links of a rusted chain.

He tries to find
the event of conception and discovers
a prehistoric field of lilies,
looks for consequence
and almost drowns in the spasms of the sea.

The chain lies all around
like the ocean, but he thinks in a straight
line and God is an arc, a whoosh
through time ascending.

People see him on the sand
and laugh, or else pull their children away—
a small demented man
digging channels to the field,
throwing flowers at the waves.

Fulton Fish Market

The curve of the island
and the smell have brought me here,
the day's fresh catch just in
from the sea

and I happen on this gathering of eyes,
heads, tails to see spines tangle
in stiff battles, pale fillets lick
boxfuls of crushed ice.

Send for the fishmonger,
ask for the meaning of fish
when they die—
bubbles of blood on the gills
like romantic poets.

In the bottom of the box
there is usually a fluttering.
I would like to believe
under all that cold
a heart fights for water.

The fishmonger loves
my whooshing from world to world
pouting at the sun
shivering with silence.

Blind hunger is the best bait

he declares proudly from his chair—
ruler of bones and salt
flesh-lord of the universe. . . .

The box is still.
The Brooklyn Bridge arches into the afterlife.

Bombing of Tyre

We've left the children out
again, torn fences down,
made caverns where the gardens
grew. Look at them watch cinders,

eyes ablaze with vacant
flames, despair. Blast me
if I know what these stones mean
except that men once shaped them

to escape. And he of stones
came passing by: "Bombs and man
the bursting heart"
then into the flashing sea.

We found this:
lust driven skyward
with our pillared dreams.
Bones of our fathers

gathering at the edge of town
where the road leads long away,
the land is lost
to the lapping waves,

the passion of the saints
maims labor with silence here
wandering in dust
for forty years.

Learn to recognize the pride
we bring to peristyles
and colonnades. It crumbles.
Learn the pieces falling.

Make room in the heart:
the moon dye spills.
So many ruins
and the sparkle of fire in boys' eyes.

Beach Haven

A string of lights bobs
on the horizon. Stars
and fishing boats collide.
Beyond the dunes the past
awaits with its mercury
and masks. Before me
is the night, the crashing
of the world.

I lie back on the sand,
bound to freedom.
The future is returning.

The Ivory Tower

It has taken a long time
and the tusks of many elephants.
It is not a conspicuous place—
straight and simple
by a calm clean river.
It is surrounded by moderate woods.
On the horizon a cloud or two
roll gently by.
Birds, of course:
hawks, thrushes, doves.
The great cliffs behind it
add mystery and the degree of solitude
by which one measures God.
Beyond the cliffs there is lightning
and barbarous armies clashing.
There is also poverty and despair
and frowns scuttling across deserts,
and all manner of sins growing
gnarled and knotted from the earth.
Do not dwell on this.
The daffodils are coming up
by the marble bench. Let us go
and pick them.

Why I Look Out Windows

I can hear
the arguments of steel, cranium
of the rains of March,
murmur of petals,
soft milk of love in solitude.
I can feel
my bones disguise themselves
in architecture, flesh and fate:
ripples across oceans
each night more vast, each year
more difficult to wake from.

I can talk to the mirrors of darkness.
They answer flickers
of starlight and ice: a voice,
a breathing across centuries,
the universe made finite in reflection.

Dawn over Washington

Everywhere institutions.
In glass bodices, in marble corsets.
What you hear
is soft-hum
            to the lavish
betrayal of fear
            and its governance.

Five AM is tender time,
                        the sun
clings to horizons
and someone kisses
            the blue stone
            of your entrails.

When the dream goes
this way and that
            you recognize
            the fountains' music:

Freedom
more alive than you.

In the Old Times

In the city where night folds its edges
into carton rows of houses,
where we lock our doors
and drown our age in prayers,
a siren passes
and fears begin to dance:
blacks smiling like razor blades,
puertoricans with small
out-of-this-nation eyes, huddling in corners,
junkies and communists and faggots
with their sequined assholes
and double-barreled pederast penises.
Listen.
Think of the old times
when all the men came home
and drank and ate and fucked
and not a word was said before
they fell in bed like sacks of smoke,
all their dreams dancing round them
like lusty children, small-eyed
women, Salomes
grunting for the pleasure of a bleeding head.
Their knives glistened with moonlight.
They ate of the head
and wet their lips with the sea.

The siren passes and fades in the bedroom.
In the old times we feared ourselves.

Two

6:40 to Trenton

All these people, trains,
evening papers, flapping ties.
All this longing for a kiss
in the darkness, flicker of candle tongue.

Rain dances in the clouds,
music drops on the arcing ground
at the end of the ride.

All the courage to swim wide flesh,
to enter the eyelid of a dream,
the country where the elements of loss
are small black birds
disappearing into blue.

View Downriver

That bridge is a poem
he said donning his jacket
as the wind whipped up the leaves.

Trenton makes.

The world
doesn't know beauty.
The river shows its teeth
ready to swallow children.

Takes
a blind eye,
a man
ready to drop at the factory door.
Balls it's cold he said.

Takes knowing
what those letters say,

a few beers
not to see the bed at night,
the wife spread open
like a crusty beach,
daughters polishing their nails
laughing at his pitted teeth.

Takes giving up,
a chance to die in peace.
No questions asked.

Cadwalader Park, Late Fall

The strollers hunch
against the wind, call to their children
from lengthening shadows.

The parents turn to each other.
More lines in the face,
more of the tinge of age.

When the man wants a kiss
his eyes open to his mate's bones,
slow of speech, eyebrows frail as horizons.

The harvest is done.
The year darkens into snow.

Crossing

A field of snow.
You can only look across it for so long.
You could go blind.
You could freeze. You could
turn back and leave it
cold and brilliant as the hand of God.
At the end you imagine a lover,
a parent, someone
who ignored you years ago.
So you throw yourself
into the field and walk, slowly at first,
feline, stalking.

Soon the anxiety becomes unbearable
like cold or brilliance. You run,
you scream, you fall, your mouth
fills with snow, you get up,
you try to weep, the field
is wider than you thought—go on,
go on, crawl if you must.

Now you're close. A few yards away
you say Surprise.
The face turns and it has your eyes,
your nose, your mouth panting,
cold and almost blind. Behind you,
at the edge of the unspoiled field,
a dim figure stamps its feet—
parent, lover, someone,
acres of snow between you.

Sam's Deli, South Broad

The tall man with the hair
cut straight across the forehead
lounges smoking cigarettes.

You don't even get a napkin
with your hamburger.

I remember a girl long ago
I made love to with my socks on.

Some twist of life
brought Sam, bristled and chubby,
to this landmark of grease
in the gut of Trenton.

The tall man asks for a Klondike
bar, then the usual for lunch.

I remember the bitter cold outside
and her gasps like a bellows on the couch.

A cat drifts among styrofoam towers.
Love was surrender then, and now

South Broad, no napkin, ketchup
dripping out of the bun.

Iron Dust

This close to spring
there is no more news
worth waiting for under
the light of the 7/11 parking lot.

No truth beyond
the dirty blond boy
slapping the video game
by the charcoal bags
or the tee-shirted enormity
of the cashier's breasts,
milk in the cooler,
Playboy, Hot Rod, Hustler,
Easy Rider, Sporting News.

And the fog is white
not yellow, and it's
more like breath not
a cat, more like stomach,
like the soul of a man
who went to hell on a dare
and touched the underknee of God.

North is Calvintown.
South is Trenton,

Route 31,
all the stations
closed or closing, the car
out of gas running on hope
and the convenient coffee
like iron-dust soup.

The Lathe of Navels

The massage parlor is old and beaten;
the girl pretends to be a poet
with her crooked mouth and her toothy grin.
Did it ever occur?

You swallow. It is acid
at first but somehow like children
words settle.

Wait, this is a highbrow place,
even the toilet salesman speaks
of grand events. His voice
hasn't changed at all since
Princeton, 1967. Has it?

Coming to terms with emptiness,
making it sweet as it trickles
down the throat.

The dreadful face of failure
is always staring out of a corner
the black waiter has just passed.

The problem is that some of the children
will not dance. Some of the children
have club feet or gnarled hands,
some die of fright before you.

Are you to freeze and starve,
are you to run to the nearest cave
and curse your knowledge of phrenology?
Are you to scream because the emptiness
has yielded nothing but dried blood?
The dreadful face, did it ever occur?

On the coffee table is a book
that illustrates pressure points,
the movement of hands on undulating skin,

machines that help, salves for lubrication,
an erotic appendix at the end.

We all make do
when hope disappears:
hors d'oeuvre, the female poet
out of work searching for God
in the parlor, the bare back
gleaming into an edible consistency.

State Complex

Steeples rise with chimneys and bureaucracies
to dim the sun. The river is forgotten, horizontal.
The city lavishes upon itself the clarity of numbers.
The temples resemble offices, the offices
resemble prisons, the prisons resemble factories.
After all these years and marble steps
only the river knows where it goes.
Or cares not following the pull of accidence.

In the park I think of ancient Chinese poets
so distant from the stains of history.
They knew their fallacies and drank their wine
while winds wore pavilions down to stone
and scattered the imperial dreams of permanence
they celebrated.

Wisp of death. Ripple of rapids and curve of light
over the bank. At dusk the weeds and garbage
gain distinction. The structures hum in Sunday rest,
yellow like urine or gold. God a huge cat slinks
through parking lots and autumn strokes the avenues.
It is cold. The night pours out like water.

Palm Sunday

Oil slicks the back of morning. Trees
bend with the weight of ten o'clock. Dead faces
come scurrying past closed gates over and under
barbed wire to dead earth where sleep unfolds
and children roam with nothing to do.

God doesn't sleep in the heavens. God doesn't search
for uproarious joy. The men in glass towers
accomplish more than a boy who nails a crucifix
on his wall.

Inscrutable face of twenty centuries, eight-legged
riddle with wings and posthumous surgings,
the hole I've dug in search of you has left
me upside down and kicking, lips to wormy dirt.
Nothing will save me from your stone disease,
your population of shadows, your million copper suns:
empty wind, dead earth.

Rather a song about daisies, rather the boy
gathering snakes by the tail, rather the obese
virgin in the restaurant demanding cake, more cake,
and the president obliging, and the farmers in Kansas
planting more wheat, and priests offering
encapsulated absolutions and pain repellent. Asterisk
of Aryan ostensibles. Emmanuel of the Golden Promises!
You have made it! You have stropped the river
till it shines and tied our dreams to this dead earth
where the huge bird Freedom spreads its wings!

October

I walk into a field of cat grass and weeds,
clumps of trees, rubble.
I people the field with memories of ancient wars,
focus on a peasant with a club foot walking home.

I think of someone who came to me
in a dream hoping to start over
and I was cold like the wind that rips
across the flatlands bringing snow
and its silence, a tuft or two
of grass sticking through the ice.

The field is in New Jersey. There are no peasants
here; no battle-weary ghosts rise from the ground.
There is a face I can barely remember.

Miles away on the right factories belch their smoke
and a steel bridge carries trucks over a channel.
They say the field stretches to the sea and almost
touches the waves. I cannot see that far.

Betrayal

This alphabet of one sensibility
                    —Kenneth Rexroth

The young man sits across from me
in the library
and writes a poem to a girl.

He has not seen her
since she left him waiting
in her living room.

Your sister, he writes, she too
loved you but was afraid.
Come back Mirelle,
come back to my arms.

He pauses. I write.
He reads. I look away.

It was a Saturday in autumn.
When she arrived
five hours late
the world had turned
the color of her eyes.

Pablo Medina

Littoral

Shadows stain the sea,
change the waves' direction,
call up mackerels
to the shoulders of burned saints.

Curly girls dance on the shore
and etch the future under clouds
like pennants and pianos exploding.

An old man raises his arms
arcwise overhead. He does an entrechat
before he looks to sails,
young things in the sun,
tacking away from the dunes.

Jersey Nights

CAMDEN

for James Haba

Something secret raced down the street
and left a smell behind—
a rose in heaven, a cat long dead.

Someone hung intestines from electric lines,
nuzzled a gravestone,
tasted the ashes of apple pies.

I saw boys straddled on fences
looking for manhood
and women with eyes for pigeons.
Their brains were full of knives,
their hearts were full of feathers.

In Camden just under the wind
I heard the sighs of an old poet waking.
He sensed the meaning of chimneys,
he sang until the factories whimpered
and the willows turned up their branches
and the ruins turned to butterflies.

NEWARK

for Francesca Skoczylas

Out of the marsh,
out of the center of the functions
of things, out of the arcing roadway
and the roaring trucks, out of the drainpipe
as the snow melts and purifies the dark,
out of the itchy poets and the pest
control deputies and the organized men
lounging in their dream canoes and ladies

in fur coats dripping with mustard, out
of the blue light of blindness, the city rises

gorged on best intentions, sucking
the teat of the mother of dawn,
Newark of a little laughter, a little
light, a little beer on the stoop,
a little jazz in the stairwell,

Newark hoping for some rain, some flood
left over, grateful of the work
that fills the spaces between love,
facing the spot where the sun rises,
where the sea makes waves, where a girl
sucking on a lollipop is looking down the boulevard.

TRENTON

for Joseph Szabo

Deep winter night.
The tongues of the Commons quivered—
the salt tongues
and the bitter tongues,
the tongues of the dreams of Hungarians,
the tongues of widows sealing envelopes
for their husbands,
tongues of macadam,
pine barren tongues,
tongues of poets and politicians
battling each other with mirrors.

I met a woman
cradling a stone in her arms.
The doctor found it by her bladder
waiting for light.
She walked on singing.
Her talisman cracked.

When the snows come
they stay for days,
when the snows leave
the night wounds heal.

The highways point
to states of concrete,
waves, golden corn.

Love, the nest under rushes
by the ice-jammed river.

Three

To the Muse

Here on your nape is the thinnest vein
where meaning gathers. Here on your shoulders
is the sweat of summer. I taste it like wine,
like sleep. There is no mend to winter's tear,
there is no end to this tomorrow.

I am tired of waiting. And I am tired
of watching the moon spill on my hands.
I am tired of my bones in the morning,
the monotone of work and wires.

Once there were no sounds and the earth
rested round and satisfied. The river spoke
the language of wells and loam or none at all.

I grow deaf on purpose. The moon is mother to my age:
there could be love but it would be a word.
There could be hope and it would be
a mouth or milk or briers.

The answer is a stone, a city of locked doors,
the storm in your breast turned fog and in the fog
dead coal and in the night a mouthful of ashes.

Every road leads out.
Bed gathers dust and fish swim up the stair.
I'll go. That's all. The greener side
of dreams is in the world. Your vein leads there.

Poetics

To the left is
the left.
Above is above.
The curtain flutters.
Behind it
to the right is
to the right of
behind the curtain.
Above below
and in between
the left
and right of
behind the curtain
is not in front.
The wind enters.
So soft,
it is so soft!

Friendship as Cinematic Fantasy

This friendship grows
becomes a breast between us.

It is the hand
sloping toward the nipple
soft electric
that glows as distance
milky lover
with a hatful of stars
there is beginning
always in pink
the lush occasional
oil of words glistens it
makes it pretty

like the starlet's
I sucked at fourteen.

Time's Winged Chariot

Now I sit calmly in the plane,
tempted to relax,
start a conversation with the fine
professional woman to the left.

Now I can run my hand
up her stockinged thigh
while she praises the National
Symphony, the Democrats' views.
Secretly I praise
the democratic vista of her calves,
monk in the cloister of desire.

A cloud goes by.
Her blouse is open to the glitters
and my heart is rattling.
Another drink.
I am getting to the point.

Her belly bulges slightly.
Who will dig the plot?
And who will mourn my passing?
The crash is imminent.
The ground below will not soften.

Oh lovely professional lady
melt on my hand.

Coney Island Stag

She smiled and coy stuck
a flower in my hair as the sun
ate California and the sea
wrinkled like a prune.

Everything turned gray called dusk
(undershirt of night)
and young men walked by
wagging floppy disks.

Thin in tight jeans,
navel kissing her buckle,
store front lovely glinted
and melted every computer in Brooklyn.

There was no antidote.
Calvin had moved to the suburbs
next to God, the Father of Philosophy
sold pizza with dark olives
and Asissi wrapped
a cassock round his motives.

When the fire spread to Brighton,
when the subway wailed for her belly,
I woke in bed with my flower panting.

Cosmology for the Beloved's Leg

Toes

They seek cover in musty leather
or nape hair. I have felt
archangel wings reaching for my brain
and I have cast out my fear.

Arch

Whoever kisses here
will taste the rainbow,
a river of veins,
dogs howling at midnight.

Ankle

This gathering of bone,
this false conclusion,
is a stark and thirsty place.
It burns my tongue.

Calf

Oh lust constellation,
philosopher's pillow,
when will you muffle
my mind's dark birds?

Knee

When the mist breaks
I see a morning seed,
the secret of the rose,
mute sorcerer of stone.

Thigh

White and ample as the moon
I follow this downy road
to the end of the known. Beyond it
stars glitter in the mouth of God.

Happiness

Out beyond the limits
I have established for myself—
trees, water, at night the moon—
someone is running errands
or doing laundry or scrubbing a bathroom.
She loves me. I keep this knowledge well.
Every night I unwrap it,
study it, pry it apart with my fingers
to find truth in the matter.
I consider myself fortunate.
I shoot cherubs across the river
where I think she is. Occasionally
one lands on target.
It seems to make a difference.
I don't know about happiness.

Landscape with a Red Bridge

Slow end
to November,
hands cold and wind-
driven, the sky
like a cow moving
west. It is gray.

Are your eyes gray
with the past? The water has an end
where it goes moving
past the nape of November.
Watch the sky,
the whorls of wind.

When the wind
touches your hair the gray
disappears, the sky
shows an end,
the edge of November.
It is moving.

My eyes are moving
round you with the wind.
I'll call this November,
dip my wings into the gray,
fly to the end
my love: the sky.

Such gold in the sky,
such a star moving
in your eyes. At the end
of the road the wind
gathers gray
with a thousand Novembers.

Two weeks ago November
blistered the sky
so gray

the veins stopped moving.
To the wind
it said: there is no end.

It is almost Christmas. November drops in the wind.
The gray cow of the sky is moving.
I walk across the red bridge to meet you at road's end.

Romance with Lights

It is warm.
A Sunday night
like a soup of presages
and crickets and clams.
A car pulls into the parking lot.
Its lights shoot across the room
and disappear.

I think of the first day,
January cold outside,
your face opening into a cloud,
a swarm of red bees. I took your hand.
My soul flapped like a sheet in the wind.

In the morning
your body was a lake flickering
with membranes and moss.

The shore was far away and dim.
The water ringed my neck:
I was bird, angel, reptile.
In you I flew, I swam,
I spurted water like a whale,
I searched the bottom for your roe
and when I broke the surface with my gasp
the sky was there, the sun,
the breeze of your breath.

It is night
and I sweat and you are
all the way across the darkness.
My skin smells of fear—
of the slough that drowns the will
and petrifies the heart,
of standing on the shore
without fins or wings or mouth,
of a car that drives into the parking lot
and kills the light.

Mala suerte

All this water comes to the door
with a voice like a French gentleman's.
Excuse me, I have petals in my throat.

My feet chase after you
to the end of Route 95.
The lilies wilt.
Solitude is a dark rain
between me and the river.

By Go the Geese Tonight

By go the geese tonight,
by goes your body arching
like twilight at dusk,
So much has passed,
so much that could have been
now lies dark as death.
By goes the wing of your smile.
It becomes the horizon.
It becomes the night,
distant and unspoken.
The door closes softly, like snow.
The heart coils against the cold,
it grows a scar.
The only sound geese flying home.

The River at Watermead

Out by the river it used to be
magnolias scented the air and your name
dropped among the petals.
A bitter wind lashes my cheeks,
a crow rests on the bare branches.
This silence wakes me:
I am alone.

Return to Dumbarton Oaks

But once you made the night
stop before our eyes,
sitting by broken trees
and dying flowers you
were the rose we whirled around.

Now we have come back,
joyous and drunken still
on the liquor of that November wind
we drank and turned to wings.

Yellow rain
boxwood and woodruff

the huge mansion of memory.

It is late summer. The chrysanthemums
flame and the trees lunge skyward
like green smoke.

Somewhere in elegant rooms
the white powder of tedium
bleaches you.

I Am Going to Sleep

I am going to ask the angels' reprieve
just this one night, for the sake of old times,
for the future's blank wall, its fissures
stuffed with hay. Let everyone know me
by the pure love of sewers, of the soul's
dark nights, of the neighbor dragging home
the bones of his wife.

I am going to curl, cover my head, say no
to mercury and siren songs,
deaf to train hoots and trucks
churning visions through the screaming night.

Give me a blanket, a corner of softness.
Give me a room where my father's lies
are forgotten and no nine year old lusts
for his mother and no roaches wiggle their whiskers
at wise men. Tell everyone I want no money,
no magazines or lofty appeals or hellos
or music played from the cornices of art.
I want to lie with death's cousin.

I am going to sleep.

Madame America

1. *Privy*

Midnight he entered
the dream shore where oceans pounded
and fish puckered for the kiss of maidens.

Midnight and his bladder sang.
Finished, too
tired to revel in relief,
he pushed the lever, saw Hades mouth
fill quicker than it could swallow,
dribble over icy lips
down stony chin to toes:
islands, minnows in tidal waste,
stunned amphibians.

2. *Poker*

She lay on a crimson recliner,
languorous, fully dressed. Her caftan
swelled with every breath. The candle
flickered and he thought of Jewish Alps,
Shoshone burial mounds. . . .
Outside hyacinths were blooming,
peonies were up.

His last card was the ace of clubs.
Her white feet arched, the night
was hers. She wagered all: her clothes,
the fillets on her hair, her crescent
custom pin. He stiffened. She yawned.
The room was still. A scent of lilac
and musk tarnished the air.

"Do you call me or raise?"
She mocked his scant manuring.

When the moon broke
and the eel's fast ended she showed her hand.

Landscape, bare yourself!

3. *Spanish Lesson*

"Ven" he said accented
but impervious. "Dame lo que das."

Water she,
sluicing water,
sent him headlong
to despair where he wallowed
till he woke.

She went home
with wallet and watch.
Day's work for day's wages.

Joseph the last of his names,
he made his choice:
clean teeth and the radiance of failure.
"Death will wear me smiling."

4. *Next-to-Last Supper*

He cooked horizons.
Star tongues slapped
the roof of night.

He lived insouciant to the end
and listened to the neighbor's dogs
yelping at the heels of time.

The pan of his thought lay idle,
lard of memory popping,
insomnia the flame.

The breeze was tar, the evening
on its steel bed sighed
for the mothers of dawn.

He closed his eyes and his hunger died
and he sank to where the fish sleep
and the earth cries.

5. *Deluge*

Under the pillow was sand,
splinters from an ancient tree,

centuries of syntax,
syllables of land, pruned mind,
heart in brine.

Words fell apart,
turned Babel babe hell
tongue slither grunt
Calliope.

The angels of Freedom
gathered pieces with the up
side down
and let the punctuation loose

touch me
rub my knee
one
last
blessed
time

Après moi

Spring Days

Spring days come to me
like a dose of God's breath: hills,
birds, boys throwing balls
all afternoon. Cobwebs sparkle,
the mist clears. Snow is a dim memory
that almost smothered hope.
I forget this was a poem to explain
the dirges, the howls out of the wind;
this was a poem to make her love me.
It is hard to return to dreams
once startled out of them. Sometimes
the jaw of night clamps on the nape
and will not let go. Today is flower
and vine twirling about my leg.
She is lost beyond the river
where trucks devour children.
Whirls of petals fly round my bed.

Lilacs in Bloom

Baby land
　　　　who told you to grow fangs?
　　　　Who streaked your skin with
　　　　　　　　　　　　smears of this
　　　　　　　　　　　　smears of that?
Purple lipped
bottom blued.
　　　　　This is the place
　　　　　This is the place
　　　　　This is the place
　　　　　　　　　　I lost my sense.

　　　　　Baby land

I'm not to blame
　　　　　the king has gone into hiding
　　　　　the queen has gone into hiding
　　　　　the princes, presidents, prime ministers,
　　　　　the bishop and his retinue
　　　　　　　　　　　　gone into hiding,
Baby land I'm not.

　　　　　　　*　　*　　*

Chaos is not to be considered. Darkness
is not to be considered or cold or heat or
ambergris muezzins castration St. Jerome
the urchin planes spilling out of the sky
madonnas traffic circles locomotives absinthe
polymers the beautiful brains of poets
spilled among the poppies babushkas bagels
manganate the dizzying heartaches of the young
destroyed by love or its absence a petard in
the ear a petard in the ear dromedarians
crossing the forehead Aristotle's vision clouded
over by the virgin's prothalamian ecstasy
rhododendron fever in the morning Godiva
salivations calamities in Kansas the philosopher's

stone passed on from alchemist father
to alchemist son to alchemist fetus
dropped in pieces on the mother's belly
a host of pigs scurrying up and down glass
corridors ha ha the separation of church and state
the separation of life and death the separation
of man and woman the separation of light and dark
father and son boredom and dog food maggots and angina
separation separation separation separation oh
Baby land your shadows suck us in quicker than we
can close our eyes to see the comet of death
come right through to the final coma
quicker than breath quicker than scream quicker
than the soul drowns in the glue of life. Ha ha.

*   *   *

I have wept all this night
I have wept ten thousand times the rain
                              the beauty of spring
flat against the darkness
                    I walk in dread
like a horse led to death
                    I wait for nothing
                    I rest for nothing.

A soft wind blows away the petals
a sorrow as wide as the river
                        beside me.

*   *   *

My luv is like a red red

                    Who said that?
                    And after I brush my teeth
                    I have breakfast and then I dress
                    and go to work. It is what I do
                    all day.

So said Mr. Turner whose soul is sense

                              whose strength is
                                        as
                                        the
                                        strength
                                        of
                                        ten.

                         *   *   *

Sun sweat
            moon tears
civilizations
            bred in gold
mendicant coins
                 clinking
with the mind-
                 lessness of gold
language
         for the greater glory of gold
                              (with annuated lisps
                               through teeth
                               of gold)
lover of gold

            the rings of holy men
            glisten for you
            the temples erect
            and ancient for you
            the saints in the mountains
            the geese honking
                         for you:

                         Listen!

When I see spring coming
a violin a violin
when I see the spider
crawl across the window pane
oh skin

Pablo Medina

when I see the river flow like sleep
my lover's arm
spread on the sheets of her solitude

                                    I want no more.

Could it be that love
makes sense because it doesn't even if the angels
pound my belly every night with billy clubs
until it is dark and swollen

dawn
        a flutter of wings.

All the cotton in the world
                        couldn't fill the

. They operated:
                found an ocean of gall
                stones as big as the moon
                                    teeth too

and the lips of a woman.
                        Lo!

Lilacs in bloom.

Four

Propaedeutics for a Season of Change

for my grandmother, 1899-1985

Juana died last week
just as weather warmed.

The forsythia sprouted
little yellow fingers.

I heard the first woodpecker
working up a tree

and the afternoon filled
with flapping sheets.

Juana died last week.
The daffodils were dancing.

Remembering

for Luis Aragón Dulzaides

At first he would forget—
a man of such mammoth memory
he knew whole novels by heart—
who that person was
who stopped to visit every day,
when his birthday came and passed,
how to get home from the store.
After his mind's collapse
his feet forgot to walk,
his muscles to hold back his wastes
(the flushing toilet made him laugh).
Bedridden the body
forgot it was a body, curled
into itself, the skin
a thin disguise on the bones,
returned to beginnings, ready for death,
the next meal tubed into it.

My son asked me by the door,
"What's the funny smell?"
And I was dumb remembering.

The Beginning

I don't know the name
where all this started:
a gathering of stone and jagged peaks,
silence like mist disguising distance.
I came to it thinking I could make my fire
glow off the moon.
There were myths, dragons' teeth,
the shadows of mute crows.
Then I tasted rose in my throat,
murmur of a growing rust.
I saw a child walking away
through mountains. I thought
he turned but it could have been
my need contriving or someone
who told me years later he must have.
I remember the planks of the world
dropping and the rain seeping
down roots to the dark bone.

Nocturne

There is wind in the trees,
black sound of owls under stars:
I return to the motions of the seas.

The moon slips through the waves,
la antigua relación entre palabra y musgo.
The wind rails at the trees,

what first gave light to incense
and myrtle at the entrance to shadows—
I return there always

to the brunt of bone that spawns the arteries
of summer, spider to its bed,
the wind to its image in the trees.

Thin-legged so the evening is,
green leaves flailed by weather
and the motions of the seas.

Dangerous and loving, old as death,
antigua araña: palabra, musgo, sleep and fire.
Wind in the trees!
I return to the motions of the seas.

Cuban Lullaby

The throat is tight. Palm trees in the gut.
El borde de la mentira:
memory all the same and laces of laughter.

Try to define it, this search, this
languor between languages, hunger
to leave one's skin, to find freed flesh
prettier than the breeeze.

The girl with the wide hips wades into the sea,
coconut milk in her groin, lilac
lips as close to truth as ever were.
The boot black on the boulevard would
spill his rum over that waist the water rings.
She wades into the sea,
lost to the taste-bleared tongue.

The Daughter of Memory

Long time ago
                on the beach
the girl in the sequined
                                swimsuit
called me behind a pillar
                                for a dime I could
see her pull the crotch
                                of the suit
to one side watch the puffy
                                hairless seam
fold on itself. I paid the price.
                                I keep on
paying it—something about
                                the communion
of silver and flesh
                                in the shadows
that's kept me here
                                all these years.

Mariposa

The butterfly, the sacred one,
flies large circles over the river
and lands on a spot
mapped out before birth,
soft as a brown feather,
too cold lengua de mar,
too dark lengua de yodo.

And so the afternoon,
a word's mad circle widening, narrowing
till a grain of sand
reaches the heart. An instant
of piercing stoppage! Needle's head,
bird's beak, the train's last call
before disappearing into the desert of memory.

The hills are barren,
the sun shines everywhere the same.
The mind slides along
the grass, glides into water,
pins itself to dreams of anywhere,
wings heavy with salt.
Clear as tropic night, mariposa,
the sacred one, cabecita negra en la maleza—
the far shore yet the thrust of hope.

Living with Shadows

Birds are singing as they have
every day since spring.
The river lazes downstream brown from rain.
They all say whoever lives here
lives in Paradise.
I've made the best of it
but the summer is short-lived.
Already the sunflowers turn face down,
I think of fall and the chill river winds.
A large moth settles on my forehead.
I will not make it move.

The Arrival

A dark bird has been flying
from shore to shore.
The river is a wide branch.
The bird will not settle.

I watch from the yard, sipping wine.
A moth has fallen into the cup.
Its wings grow heavy as I think of you.
Soon it will drown in the red night.

What the Soldier Did

Before the Fugue

My life has come to sitting
on the bones of colonels,
trying to unravel the orders they left.

That the gun-shy privates ran away
with all the ammunition is
of no consequence. The mound
will be held at all costs.

I'm the only one; therefore
the colonels have nothing to lose
but their gilded thumbnails.
Their widows sing of oranges
and southern afternoons
until they burst.

I was told not to understand.
More colonels die. The mound grows.
The jackals come at night.
And I have only bones and a ragged flag.

Rationale

I couldn't stay.
The bones were cold and loneliness
has no bearing without sorrow.

It was like pennies
on the trembling hand,
this tendon stretched to whining,
this waiting.

I, the last, left
before the fierce winds, before
the avalanche of skulls made me colonel

honorary
dead.

The women do not know
why I wake at night bleeding for their husbands.

The Histories

There was no war, no insurrection.
The colonels flew into the light
and crackled and fell to wax.

Only here and there a wail
came from mothering lips; wives
swelled seasides with varicose and daffodils
and the orders appeared:

eat a moth,
kiss live coals,
never use your tongue
except to bite on when the bullets come
or guide spittle to your boots.
Ears you are
and the feed of darkness.

Reliquary

The men are gone
who went to fire and knew
not and answered not but received
and passed on.

I wander rudderless
through continents of smoke,
through nipple rot and the dead snake's roe.
I hear the relics calling—

morning, night.
In the haze is a face,
in the face is a blackbird,
cheeks crumbling,
lips glowing like ashes.

On the Death of a Spanish Poet

In the afternoon
boys float on the river,
a horse clops on the street below,
old men hide under almonds,
the myrtle bush cries
I will not bloom
I will not bloom.

We have come for the poet.
He lifts his head from the page.
Light oozes like myrrh into corners and hardens.

Three men, green like olives,
lead him past the jalousies, past the cold
grave silence of the church
to a crumbling jail.

Why spare a poet?
The boys on the river,
jagged women in black
carting buckets of sorrow,
the elm trees, the grass,
the mare and the foal,
the bull with nostrils like October, 1936,
Granada, Granada.

They took him out of his cell,
out of the urine and fear,
and drove him to the countryside.

When the air was a rainbow of blindness and bones,
when lead made a sound like an orange on his nape,
a hundred nightingales danced in his ear
and roses raced through his veins.
All the world spilled out of him:

planets and stars, breasts,
lime-covered thighs,
almonds and myrrh
and the myrtle bush blooming in Granada.

The Exile

He returned to grass two feet tall
around the house, a rope dangling
from the oak, an absence of dogs.
The year had neither ended nor begun,
the sun had yawned away the rain
and worms were drying on the ground.

Memories floated down from the trees: cane fields,
the smokehouse and its hanging meats,
breeze of orange and bamboo, a singing at dawn.

"Will you be with me?"
The voice came from the river. The jasmine
bloomed in the garden, he hiding,
he sweating under the moon
wanting to say I will I will and more.

There were stones all over the yard smelling of time.
He picked a few, threw them down the well
and listened to the water swallowing.

It made him smaller. He walked out the gate
and closed it behind him, wiped the sweat from his eyes,
felt his feet settling on the road.

Author's Bibliography

Books

Pork Rind and Cuban Songs. Washington, D.C.: Nuclassics and Science, 1975.

Exiled Memories: A Cuban Childhood. Austin, TX: University of Texas Press, 1990.

Everyone Will Have to Listen / Todos me van a tener que oír: The Poetry of Tania Díaz Castro. (Ed. & Trans. with Carolina Hospital.) Princeton, NJ: Linden Lane Press/Ediciones Ellas, 1990.

Poems in Anthologies

"From Side to Side," "Storm Door," "The Just and Human Time," "Man at the Edge," "Out of the Game." (Translations from the Spanish of Heberto Padilla.) *Subversive Poetry.* Washington, D.C.: Georgetown University Cuban Students Association, 1972. 10, 14-15, 28.

"Fulton Fish Market," "Crossing," "The Exile," "Wrath." *US 1: An Anthology.* Roosevelt, NJ: U.S. 1 Cooperative, 1980. 103-107.

"Bombing of Tyre." *And Not Surrender: American Poets on Lebanon.* Washington, D.C.: Arab American Cultural Foundation, November 1982. 15.

"El señor perdido en las tánganas de la noche," "Elena," "Almuerzo en la hierba," "Cómo se distrae la lluvia de febrero," "La niña de los números." *El jardín también es nuestro.* New Brunswick, NJ: SLUSA, 1988. 136-138.

"Beach Haven," "The Arrival," "Cuban Lullaby," "State Complex," "Discourse on Method," "The Exile," "Nocturne." *Cuban American Writers: Los Atrevidos.* Princeton, NJ: Linden Lane Press, 1988. 61-67.

"October," "View Downriver," "6:40 to Trenton," "Sam's Deli, South Broad," "State Complex." *Blue Stones and Salt Hay.* New Brunswick, NJ: Rutgers University Press, 1990. 144-147.

Poems in Periodicals

"The Last Supper." *The Georgetown College Journal* 98.1 (1969): 4.

"Well into Summer Time Weakens," "Soliloquy at Six." *The Georgetown Quarterly* 1.1 (1970): 5.

"Caught in the Act." *The Georgetown Quarterly* 1.2 (1971): 14-15.

"Wyoming Avenue." *Poet and Critic* 6.3 (1971): 10.

"Pregunta," "Madrugada." *Septagon* 1.1 (1972): 20, 21.

"Argumento." *Romanica* 2 (1974): 20.

"The Siege of Valencia." *US 1 Worksheets* 4/5 (1975): 2.

"Winter Story," "Crossing." *US 1 Worksheets* 6/7 (1975): 5.

"Song for Marina." *US 1 Worksheets* 9 (1977): 2.

"Aubade." *Cinnamon* 5 (1977): 22.

"Critique," "Allegory," "Winter Story," "Winter Scene." *The Kelsey Review* 6.1 (1978): 47-48.

"The Rape of the Head," "Hiroshima," "Lizards and Wet Dogs." *The Princeton Spectrum* 3.35 (1978): 24.

"Mala Suerte," "Cutting Down the Beech." *The Princeton Spectrum* 3.38 (1978): 40.

"On the Death of a Spanish Poet," "For the End of Winter." *US 1 Worksheets* 11 (1978): 6.

"In the Old Times." *The Spirit That Moves Us* 4.1 (1978/79): 16.

"How Do You Know, Small Tongue." *The Madison Review* 1.1 (1979): 47.

"Romance with Lights." *Milkweed Chronicle* 1.3 (1980): 4.

"Bombing of Tyre." *Arab Perspectives* 1.6 (1980): 48.

"The Ivory Tower," "Return to Dumbarton Oaks." *Poetry* 140.2 (1982): 97.

"Nocturne." *Linden Lane Magazine* 1.4 (1982): 8.

"Living with Shadows," "Mala Suerte." *Stone Country* 10. 3/4 (1983): 27.

"The Exile," "Mala Suerte." *Terra Poetica* 2 .1/2 (1983): 65.

"Lathe of Navels." *US 1 Worksheets* 16/17 (1983/84): 12.

"Birthday," "The Goose," "Parable." *Cedar Rock* 9.2 (1984): 13.

"October." *Poet Lore* 79.1 (1984): 37.

"Cartography," "Dawn over Washington." *Contact II* 6.34/35 (1984/85): 50.

"By Go the Geese Tonight," "Poetics." *Passaic Review* 7/8 (1985): 68.

"Interpretation of Dreams." *Croton Review* 8 (1985): 11.

"Sam's Deli, South Broad." *Tar River Poetry* 25.1 (1985): 19.

"Cosmology for the Beloved's Leg." *US 1 Worksheets* 18/19 (1985): 3.

"The Gates of Hell." *The Palmetto Review* 4 (1986): 16.

"Mariposa." *Hubbub* 4.2 (1986): 12.

"The Arrival," "March 9th." *Kansas Quarterly* 19.3 (1987): 179.

"Parking Lot," "Cadwalader Drive, Late Fall," "6:40 to Trenton," "View Downriver." *Black Swan Review* 2 (1989): 20.

"The Future," "True History." *US 1 Worksheets* (1989): 3-4.

"Flight Out of Miami." *Miami Monthly* 9.9 (1989): 42.

"Driving Home." *Miami Monthly* 9.12 (1989): 49.

"Giotto's Gift," "Woman Sleeping in the Morning," "Self-Portrait," "Ana in Miami." *Paterson Literary Review* (1989): 18.

"Freedom," "Anger," "Landscape with Faucet & Phone," "Riverfront." *South Trenton Review* (1989): 13-15.

"Madame America," "The Apostate," "The Beginning," "Why I Look Out Windows," "The Daughter of Memory." *The Americas Review* 17.2 (1989): 33-39.

Other Publications

"A Manifesto of the Post-Absurd" (essay). *The Courier* 19.1 (1971): 7.

"A Look Down: Notes on the Poetry of Latin America" (essay). *Three Sisters* 1.1 (1971): 20.

"Tag Ball" (short fiction). *Three Sisters* 1.3 (1971): 4.

"Arrival" (essay). *Confrontation* 27/28 (1984): 39.

"The Limits of Criticism" (essay). *Linden Lane Magazine* 4.1 (1985): 26.

"Grandfather Pablo" (essay). *The Antioch Review* 43.2 (1985): 140-148.

"Mina," "El Guayabal" (essays). *Linden Lane Magazine* 4.3 (1985): 14-15.

"El triunfo del amor" (review of García Márquez's *El amor en los tiempos del cólera*). *Linden Lane Magazine* 5.1 (1986): 22.

"Chicago" (short fiction). *The Kelsey Review* 7.1 (1988) : 8-10.

"Inner Light" (excerpt from novel). *Cuban American Writers: Los Atrevidos*. Princeton, NJ: Linden Lane Press, 1988. 68-88.

"Dos Poetas" (essay). *Linden Lane Magazine* 8.3 (1989): 24.

"Where Are You From?" (essay). *Cuban Heritage* 3.1 (1990): 3.

Reviews, Criticism, and Interviews

"Waiting Out the Far-Away Sun: The Poetry of a Cuban Exile, Pablo Medina." Review of *Pork Rind and Cuban Songs* by Gregory Orfalea. *Margins* 28/29/30 (1976): 6-10.

"Poet's News Create Visual Pictures." Review of poetry reading. *The Rider College News* 13 April 1979: 5.

"Poetry in Motion." Interview by Loretta Sherman. *P.S.* 4 February 1981: 7.

"Poetry's Angry Muse on the Move." Review of poetry reading by Michael Kiernan. *The Washington Post* 19 September 1982, sec. E: 7.

"Poetry Attracting New Audiences." Review of poetry reading by Daniel Aubrey. *The Trenton Times* 13 September 1985. Fine Arts: 8.

"Poetic Heritage Comes to GSC." Review of poetry reading by Dave Correale. *The Glassboro Whit* 6 February 1986: 14.

"Mirbad Festival Good Experience for American Poet." Interview by Hana' Shafiq. *The Baghdad Observer* 10 December 1987. Arts: 5.

"Los Atrevidos." Mention of Pablo Medina by Carolina Hospital. *Linden Lane Magazine* 6.4 (1987): 22-23.

"The Daring Ones Display Cuban Soul." Mention of Pablo Medina by Debbie Sontag. *The Miami Herald* 9 February 1989. sec. B: 1, 3.

Acknowledgments *(continued)*

"Fulton Fish Market," "Crossing," and "The Exile" appeared in *US 1: An Anthology* (US 1 Cooperative, 1980).

"The Ivory Tower" and "Return to Dumbarton Oaks" appeared in *Poetry* (American Poetry Association, 1982).

"Bombing of Tyre" appeared in *And Not Surrender: American Poets on Lebanon* (Arab American Cultural Foundation, 1982).

"Beach Haven," "The Arrival," "Cuban Lullaby," "State Complex," "Discourse on Method," "The Exile," and "Nocturne" appeared in *Cuban American Writers: Los Atrevidos* (Linden Lane Press, 1988).

"October," "View Downriver," "6:40 to Trenton," "Sam's Deli, South Broad," and "State Complex" appeared in *Bluestones and Salt Hay* (Rutgers University Press, 1990).